The Easter Story

Stephanie Jeffs
Illustrated by John Haysom

Abingdon Press

Introduction

*T*his book tells the story of the last week in the life of a man who died when he was about thirty-three years old.

He lived nearly 2,000 years ago in a country called Palestine. His mother, Mary, gave birth to him in a stable, and as a baby he was visited by shepherds and wise men. While he was still very young, he and his parents had to escape from a jealous and angry king and become refugees in a foreign country. He grew up to be a great teacher and healer, and while he had many followers, he also had many enemies.

He claimed to be many things. He said that he had come to show people how they could know God as their Father. He taught people how to live the way God wanted them to. He said he was not the son of a carpenter called Joseph, but that he was the Son of God.

This was an amazing claim. It still is. It is a remarkable story. It is the story of a man called Jesus.

Jesus the King

MATTHEW'S GOSPEL, CHAPTER 21, VERSES 1-11

"*Hurry! Hurry!*" *shouted the woman to her husband.*

"What's the rush? What's happening? Where is everyone going?" he called.

Everywhere, people who had come to celebrate the Passover Feast were running to the dusty road that led from Bethany to Jerusalem. A crowd was gathering, a good-natured crowd. People were jostling to see what was going on, but there was no trouble, no angry shouts, no violent gestures.

"What's happening?" shouted someone who, like many others, had been carried along in the excitement.

"Jesus is coming!"

"Jesus is coming as a King! He is riding on a donkey. He is coming, just like the prophets said he would. He has come to save us!"

"Then let's welcome him as King!" cried a voice above all the others.

The crowd cheered with approval. Some pulled off their cloaks and flung them onto the dusty ground, while others cut branches from the trees and waved them high in the air.

For a moment the crowd fell silent as they saw the small figure of Jesus, riding a donkey in the distance. Then the crowd began to cheer and shout: words of triumph, words of victory, words of celebration. The crowd welcomed Jesus as a conquering hero.

"Hurrah! King Jesus!"

"Hosanna! God bless the King who has come to save us!"

"Long live King Jesus!"

Jesus Goes to the Temple

MATTHEW'S GOSPEL, CHAPTER 21, VERSES 12-15

By the time Jesus reached Jerusalem everyone knew that he had arrived. Those who had never heard of him before, now heard snatches about him. He was a teacher said some, a healer said others, a troublemaker said a few more.

The crowd followed Jesus as he made his way to the temple. The temple courtyard was busy, more like a busy street market than a place of prayer. The stallholders were trying to sell animals and birds for the traditional Jewish Passover sacrifice. The moneychangers were hoping to make high profits.

But Jesus had come to God's house to pray. He looked around at all that was going on. He knew that the money changers were cheating the people. He knew that the stall holders were more concerned with money than forgiveness. He knew that this was not what God his Father wanted.

With one movement, Jesus threw over a table, sending showers of coins high into the air. He made his way through the temple area overturning one table after another.

"God's house is supposed to be a house of prayer," he shouted, "but you have turned it into a den for thieves!"

Some slunk out of the temple courts, furious with him for what he had done.

"Who does he think he is?" they growled.

But there were many beggars at the entrance to the temple, as well as those who were blind and lame. They came to Jesus and he made them well. Those who had been blind saw the temple for the very first time, and those who had been lame ran and danced about the temple courts, praising God that they had been healed. The children joined in the celebration and shouted:

"Hurrah! God has come to save us! Hosanna!"

There were some people in the temple who did not join in the celebration. Instead they stood in the shadows whispering and plotting against Jesus.

The Jar of Perfume

MATTHEW'S GOSPEL, CHAPTER 26, VERSES 6-16

One evening Jesus and his disciples were relaxing at the home of a friend called Simon the Leper.

While they were eating their meal, a woman entered the house. She held an alabaster jar of very expensive perfume. She went up to Jesus, interrupting the meal, and gently poured the perfume over his head. The liquid slowly trickled down his hair and the sweet scent of the perfume filled the air.

The disciples were outraged.

"How thoughtless!" they said. "This perfume could have been sold for a great deal of money. The money should have been given to the poor instead of being wasted in such a way."

They waited for Jesus to react, confident that he would agree with them. But Jesus surprised them, as he often did. Gently taking the woman by the hand, he turned to his friends and spoke to them firmly.

"Stop criticizing her! This woman's actions show that she knows who I am. She has done something beautiful. She hasn't been wasteful; she has prepared me for my death. What she has done today will be remembered for years to come."

The disciples were amazed. What did all this mean?

However, one of the disciples thought differently from the rest. He knew that Jesus had enemies. He knew that the chief priests would do anything to get their hands on Jesus and destroy him. He knew he had the opportunity to make some money.

Straight away he went to the chief priests and struck a deal with them.

"How much will you give me to hand over Jesus to you?"

"The price of a slave – thirty pieces of silver," they replied.

Having agreed to the deal, he waited for an opportunity to hand Jesus over to them. The disciple's name was Judas Iscariot.

The Servant King

JOHN'S GOSPEL, CHAPTER 13, VERSES 1-20

A few days later, Jesus asked his disciples to make all the preparations to celebrate the Passover meal. They met in an upstairs room, excited that they could be together. Even Judas joined them for the occasion, still watching, still waiting for an opportunity to betray Jesus.

When everyone had arrived, Jesus took off his cloak and wrapped a towel around his waist, just like a servant.

"Whatever is he doing?" wondered the disciples.

They watched as Jesus poured water into a basin. They stared as he knelt before each of them in turn and began to wash their dirty, dusty, tired feet. They remained silent as he carried out his task, wondering why their master was doing the job of a servant.

At last Jesus came to Peter and started to wash his feet. But Peter was shocked. He leapt up.

"Why are you doing this, Master?" he cried. "You shouldn't be doing this to us. I won't let you wash my feet!"

Jesus looked deep into Peter's eyes.

"You don't realize what I am doing now, Peter, but one day you will. You must understand that if you do not let me wash you, you cannot be my friend."

Instantly Peter responded, "Then don't just wash my feet, Lord, wash my head and hands as well!"

"There is no need," replied Jesus. "I have washed you, so you are clean – although not everyone here is."

Judas squirmed. He knew that the moment he had been waiting for had almost come.

"I have just done a servant's job," continued Jesus. "If you want to follow me, you must learn to serve each other."

Judas knew that he must leave the Passover meal as soon as he could.

The Last Supper

JOHN'S GOSPEL, CHAPTER 13, VERSES 21-30 AND LUKE'S GOSPEL, CHAPTER 22, VERSES 14-23

As Jesus and his disciples ate the Passover meal, Jesus made a surprising announcement.

"One of you, one of my friends, is going to betray me to my enemies."

The disciples were horrified and looked at one another in alarm. Meanwhile Judas slipped out, unnoticed, and made his escape into the night.

When he had gone, Jesus reached across the table and picked up the loaf of unleavened bread. Holding it in both hands, he raised it up and thanked God for it. Then he pulled the bread apart and gave a piece to each of his friends.

"Eat the bread I have given you. Soon my body will be broken, just like this bread. Remember what I have just done; and when you meet again for a meal, remember me."

When they had finished eating, Jesus took a cup of wine and once again thanked God for it. Then he passed it around his friends, and they all drank from the cup.

"Drink this," he said. "This wine is a sign of God's new agreement to save you, an agreement that has to be sealed with my blood. I know that I must die and that this is all part of God's plan to save you."

The disciples looked at the broken loaf of bread and the deep red remains of the wine. They wondered what it all meant.

Jesus Alone

MATTHEW'S GOSPEL, CHAPTER 26, VERSES 31-56

The night air felt cold as Jesus and his disciples walked towards the Mount of Olives. The Passover celebration had frightened and confused them. Only days ago Jesus was being hailed as a King; now he was talking of dying.

"All of you will leave me," said Jesus. "But when I have risen, I will meet up with you in Galilee."

"I won't ever leave you!" cried Peter. "I will always stand by you."

"No, you won't, Peter," replied Jesus. "Before morning you will say that you do not know me three times."

They made their way to the Garden of Gethsemane.

"Sit down and wait for me, while I go and pray," Jesus said. They sat in silence, and watched while Jesus walked deeper into the garden, with Peter, James and John as companions.

"Stay and keep awake with me," Jesus asked his friends.

Jesus went still further into the garden. He cried out to his Father, "Please save me from all the suffering that lies ahead. But if that is not possible, do what must be done, because more than anything else, I want what pleases you."

Feeling deep sorrow, Jesus went back to his friends. But he found that they had fallen asleep. "Couldn't you stay awake with me for one hour?" he asked. Jesus went away for a second time to pray, and then a third. Each time he returned to find the disciples fast asleep.

Then through the darkness came the flickering light of torches. The disciples, terrified, stumbled to their feet with their hearts pounding. Jesus stood waiting for the men who were armed with clubs and swords. At the head of the crowd was Judas Iscariot.

Judas walked straight up to Jesus. "Greetings, Rabbi," he said as he kissed his cheek.

The signal had been given. The men rushed forward and seized Jesus. He made no move to escape. The disciples fled into the darkness.

Jesus the Prisoner

LUKE'S GOSPEL, CHAPTER 22, VERSES 54-62

The arrest was quickly carried out. The prisoner did not protest in any way as they led him to the house of Caiaphas, the high priest.

The disciples had vanished, but Peter followed the crowd at a safe distance, right up to Caiaphas' house. Pulling his cloak over his head, Peter entered the courtyard and sat down with some of the soldiers, hoping to learn anything he could about Jesus.

He sat and listened. He watched and listened. Jesus was on trial... the chief priests wanted to have him killed. They could find no evidence against Jesus... he had done nothing wrong.

Straining to hear any information he could, Peter failed to notice a servant girl looking at him. He jumped when she spoke.

"You know Jesus, don't you? You were with him!"

The soldiers stationed in the courtyard stopped talking as they waited for Peter's answer.

"I don't know what you are talking about," he said, and stood up to leave the courtyard, pulling his cloak tightly around his face.

"He was with Jesus," shouted another girl, pointing her finger at him accusingly.

"I don't know anyone by that name," shouted Peter, trying to stifle the feelings of panic and fear growing inside him.

"You must be one of Jesus' friends. You speak with a Galilean accent. You must know him!" said someone else.

Peter turned and faced his accuser and shrieked with anger.

"You don't know what you are talking about! I don't know this man Jesus. I've never known Jesus! Don't you understand?"

He backed off, ready to make his escape. Somewhere a cock crowed. A new day had begun. Peter remembered what Jesus had said. He had betrayed his friend.

The Crown of Thorns

JOHN'S GOSPEL, CHAPTER 19, VERSES 1-17

Meanwhile there had been an unsatisfactory trial at Caiaphas' house. Unable to find any real evidence against Jesus, the high priest had accused him of blasphemy and had become so angry that he had ripped his clothes in fury. So, the elders decided to hand Jesus over to Pilate, the Roman Governor. Perhaps he would be able to deal with him.

It was the last thing Pilate wanted to do. The chief priests and leaders were out to get Jesus. No amount of reason would calm them down. It was also the Passover Festival. Pilate knew he could have a riot on his hands. He didn't want that.

Jesus stood before Pilate and Pilate questioned him. Jesus remained silent. Pilate was amazed. He went to the crowd.

"It is your custom to free a prisoner at Passover. Do you want me to release Jesus, the King of the Jews?"

The chief priests and the elders acted swiftly. They whipped up the crowd into a frenzy.

"Crucify him! Crucify him!" they screamed.

The chief priests were delighted. Frightened of the crowd's reaction, Pilate gave in. He handed Jesus over to be crucified.

The soldiers jumped into action. They dressed Jesus in a purple robe, just like a king, and to complete the job they twisted together a crown of thorns and set it on his head.

Then they amused themselves by jeering at him.

"Your Majesty!" they sneered. "King of the Jews!"

They knelt before him in mock respect. They spat in his face. They laughed and sniggered.

When they had had enough, they made him carry a wooden crossbeam on his back, and led him up the hill called Calvary to die.

Crosses on a Hillside

LUKE'S GOSPEL, CHAPTER 23, VERSES 32-43 AND JOHN'S GOSPEL, CHAPTER 19, VERSES 25-30

A small crowd followed as Jesus was led out with two other men. Both of them had committed crimes punishable by death.

When they reached the top of the hill, each prisoner was nailed to his crossbeam. The crossbeams were then hoisted up into the air and attached to the poles already sunk in the ground. Jesus was in the middle, with one criminal on either side.

The people who stood at the foot of the cross were there for different reasons. Some were there to mourn; some to jeer and laugh. Jesus looked at the crowd, some of whom had nailed him to the cross.

"Father, forgive these people," Jesus said. "They don't know what they have done."

"I know who you are," shouted one of the criminals hanging next to him. "You are that man called Jesus. You said you were God's Son. Well, prove that you are by saving yourself now!"

"Be quiet!" said the other criminal. "You and I deserve to die for what we have done. But this man is innocent. He has done nothing wrong." He strained his head towards Jesus. "Remember me when you come into your kingdom."

"You will be with me today," promised Jesus.

Near the foot of the cross stood a group of women, quietly weeping. One of them was Jesus' mother, Mary. John, one of Jesus' disciples, was also nearby.

Jesus called out to his mother, "Think of John as your son." And to John he said, "Treat Mary as your mother."

At last Jesus knew that he was ready to die. With one final breath he called out to God, "Father, it is over! I have done what you wanted!"

At that moment the sky turned black. Jesus was dead.

Jesus is Alive!

JOHN'S GOSPEL, CHAPTER 20, VERSES 1, 11-16

It was a good and faithful man called Joseph, from a town called Arimathea, who saw that Jesus was buried. He gave Jesus the rock tomb he had bought for himself.

On the first day of the week, after the Passover holiday, Mary Magdalene went to the garden where the tomb was. She wanted to prepare Jesus' body for burial according to the Jewish custom. Mary was unsure how she would get to the body because a large rock had been placed across the entrance of the tomb.

The garden was still and empty as she walked towards the tomb.

Mary stopped. The rock that had stood at the entrance to the tomb had been rolled away. The tomb was empty! Jesus' body had gone! Someone must have stolen it, she thought.

Mary slumped down on the ground and tears started to fall down her cheeks. Then she saw something gleaming from within the tomb. Cautiously she looked inside. Sitting where Jesus' body had been were two angels. "Why are you crying?" they asked.

"Because they have taken away the body of my friend Jesus, and I don't know where they have put him," she wept.

She heard a noise behind her and turned round. A man was standing there. Mary thought he must be the gardener.

"Where have you put his body?" she asked.

The man looked into her eyes, and spoke her name. "Mary."

Mary recognized the voice immediately. The man was Jesus! He was not dead, he was alive, walking and talking to her in the garden! She stretched out her arms to greet him. "Teacher!" she cried in amazement.

Seeing is Believing

JOHN'S GOSPEL, CHAPTER 20, VERSES 19-29

The news that Jesus was alive soon spread among his friends. The disciples were still in Jerusalem, but they were too frightened to move for fear of what might happen to them.

One night, the majority of them met together and locked the doors for safety. But then the unexpected happened – Jesus appeared among them! The disciples were overjoyed! They were thrilled to see Jesus again. Everyone forgot their fear and enjoyed being in Jesus' company once more.

Everyone, that is, except for Thomas.

Thomas was not there when Jesus appeared to the others, and he refused to believe that Jesus was alive.

"I'll only believe that Jesus is alive when I can actually see him for myself," he said stoutly. "I won't believe until I put my own fingers into the holes where the nails were."

A week later, all the disciples met together in one room. They locked the doors, still fearful that they, too, might be arrested. From nowhere, Jesus appeared before them.

"Peace be with you," Jesus said. Then he turned and looked at Thomas. "Thomas," he said. "Look at my hands. Put your fingers in the holes where the nails were. Don't doubt any more. Believe in me."

Thomas sank to his knees, overwhelmed by what he had seen.

"You are my Lord and my God," he said. "I do believe in you."

Breakfast on the Beach

JOHN'S GOSPEL, CHAPTER 21, VERSES 1-14 AND ACTS, CHAPTER 1, VERSES 4-8

The disciples did not want to stay in Jerusalem. They knew Jesus was alive. They decided to go home, back to the Sea of Galilee. After all, Jesus had said that he would meet them there.

One night, Peter and some of the other disciples decided to go fishing. They went out in their boat and fished all night, but as light dawned they had still not caught a single fish. Then they saw a man standing on the shore. He called out to them, "Have you caught any fish, my friends?" His voice travelled across the lake.

After they had shouted back their answer, the man replied, "Throw your nets over the right hand side of the boat, and you will catch some fish."

The disciples were tired and weary of the long night's unsuccessful fishing, but they cast their nets one last time.

Almost as soon as the nets hit the water, they swelled and bulged with fish. John looked out across the water to the stranger on the beach. "It is the Lord!" he cried out.

Immediately, Peter leapt up, threw himself into the water and swam to the shore, while the others followed in the boat.

They found Jesus, sitting on the beach, waiting for them. There was a small fire, and he was cooking some fish. They shared breakfast together and Jesus talked with his friends.

Over the next forty days, Jesus appeared to his disciples many times. He then returned to heaven, to be with God, his Father. But Jesus did not leave his disciples alone. He told them to return to Jerusalem and to wait. For the Holy Spirit was to come and always be with them. The Holy Spirit would comfort them, help them, and give them the power to live as Jesus had done.

And the disciples wanted to tell everyone the good news.

A Tamarind Book
Published in the United States of America by
Abingdon Press
PO Box 801
Nashville, TN 37202-0801
U.S.A.
ISBN 0-687-08740-6

First edition 1997

Printed and bound in Singapore

The LAND and the PEOPLE

RUSSIA

CATH SENKER

Gareth Stevens
PUBLISHING

Please visit our website, www.garethstevens.com.
For a free color catalog of all our high-quality books,
call toll free 1-800-542-2595 or fax 1-877-542-2596.

CATALOGING-IN-PUBLICATION DATA

Names: Senker, Cath.
Title: Russia / Cath Senker.
Description: New York : Gareth Stevens Publishing, 2017. | Series: The land and the people |
Includes index.
Identifiers: ISBN 9781482450958 (pbk.) | ISBN 9781482450972 (library bound) |
ISBN 9781482450965 (6 pack)
Subjects: LCSH: Russia (Federation)--Juvenile literature.
Classification: LCC DK510.23 S46 2017 | DDC 947--dc23

Published in 2017 by
Gareth Stevens Publishing
111 East 14th Street, Suite 349
New York, NY 10003

Copyright © 2017 Wayland, a division of Hachette Children's Group

Editors: Nicola Edwards
Design: Dave Ball and Angela Ball at D&A
Cover design: D&A
Map artist: Stefan Chabluk

Picture acknowledgements: All images and graphic elements courtesy of Shutterstock except
p6bl and p33bWikimedia Commons, p6br, p9br, p18t, p23br, p30bl, p34b, p36br, p36r, p41t
and p43b Corbis

Printed in the United States of America
CPSIA compliance information: Batch CS16GS: For further information contact
Gareth Stevens, New York, New York at 1-800-542-2595.

CONTENTS

RUSSIA ON THE MAP

Russia is vast. The largest country on Earth, it covers over one-ninth of Earth's land and stretches across Europe and Asia. Russia has dense forests, high mountain peaks, sandy beaches and snowy winter landscapes.

Highs and lows

Over the last century, Russia has endured massive shocks: huge loss of life in both world wars, revolution, civil war, famine, and the birth of the Soviet Union, the first communist country. It has experienced industrialization at a furious pace, government terror and the complete collapse of the communist system. Yet Russia has been a world leader in culture, sports and space exploration. Since 1991, it has risen from the ashes of the Soviet Union to become one of the richest and most powerful countries in the world.

Russia fact file

Population: 142,423,773 (July 2015 est.)

Area: 6.56 million square miles (17 million sq km)

Capital city: Moscow

Highest peak: Mount Elbrus—18,510 feet (5,642 m)

Main language: Russian, written in Cyrillic alphabet

Currency: ruble

Norwegian Sea

NORWAY

FINLAND

RUSSIA
LITHUANIA
LATVIA
ESTONIA

POLAND

BELARUS

Moscow

UKRAINE

KAZAKHSTAN

GEORGIA

AZERBAIJAN

Whistle-stop Russia

A few things to do on a trip to Russia...

⌃ Go to the Bolshoi Ballet in Moscow.

⌃ Travel in style on the Trans-Siberian railway.

⌃ Enjoy a snowy horse-drawn sleigh ride.

⌃ Relax at the Black Sea coast.

Arctic Ocean

《 Russia has borders with 14 countries and the longest coastline in the world, running along part of the Arctic and Pacific oceans and 14 seas.

Sea of Okhotsk

R U S S I A

Pacific Ocean

CHINA

Sea of Japan

MONGOLIA

NORTH KOREA

CHINA

A TUMULTUOUS HISTORY

From the 16th to the 20th century, Russia was an enormous empire ruled by tsars (emperors). At the peak of society was a tiny group of wealthy people, while the great majority eked out a miserable living on the land. In 1917, the tsar was overthrown in the Russian Revolution. In 1922, Russia formed a group of republics called the Union of Soviet Socialist Republics (USSR).

⌃ Vladimir Lenin, a leader of the Russian Revolution

Stalin: "man of steel"

The new communist government aimed to create a fairer society. But by 1929 Joseph Stalin had seized almost total power. He forced the USSR to build industries at an astonishing pace and seized farmers' land, making them join collective (shared) farms.

>> Soviet tanks fighting the Germans in World War II

《 Stalin. Anyone who opposed him came to a nasty end — he used his secret police force to murder his enemies.

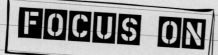

FOCUS ON

☑ COLD WAR

The communist countries were enemies of the United States and other democracies. They didn't fight each other directly but by backing the opposite sides in conflicts in other lands—this was the Cold War.

Soviet superpower

The Russian people fought heroically in World War II, helping to defeat Nazi Germany. After 1945, the USSR became a superpower, setting up communist governments in the eastern European countries it now controlled. The communist system fell in 1989, and in 1991, the USSR split into 15 independent countries. The new Russian Federation kept most of the resources but its economy nose-dived in the 1990s. The economy bounced back by the early 2000s.

AFTER COMMUNISM, RUSSIA BROUGHT BACK THE OLD NATIONAL FLAG FROM BEFORE COMMUNIST TIMES AND ADOPTED A BRAND-NEW NATIONAL ANTHEM.

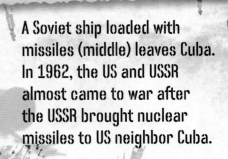

A Soviet ship loaded with missiles (middle) leaves Cuba. In 1962, the US and USSR almost came to war after the USSR brought nuclear missiles to US neighbor Cuba.

RUSSIA'S MELTING POT

Although four-fifths of the population are Russian, more than 120 ethnic groups live in Russia, most from neighboring countries. It's partly because under Soviet rule, people moved around the USSR to work, often marrying locals and raising families. After 1991, some moved back to their birth country but others stayed in their adopted land.

Population fall

Russia's population fell dramatically in the 1990s, from 149 million in 1991 to 143 million in 2010. People were having fewer children, and Russian men have a particularly low life expectancy—many drink far too much alcohol, which damages their health.

» Homelessness soared in the 1990s and remains a problem.

Famous Russians

Piotr Ilich Tchaikovsky (1840-93), composer

Leo Tolstoy (1828-1910), writer, author of *War and Peace*

Garry Kasparov, chess player

Anna Kournikova, tennis player, former model, trainer

8

RUSSIA HAS MORE IMMIGRANTS THAN ANY OTHER COUNTRY EXCEPT THE US.

Immigrants

People have flocked to Russia to fill the gaps in the workforce, working on building sites, in markets and restaurants. While most are from the former USSR, others journey from China and the poorer lands of Central Asia, seeking a better life.

≪ Migrants from Central Asia often labor on building sites.

FOCUS ON

☑ PARENTAL GLORY

From 2009, the population started to rise again. The government has brought in healthy lifestyle programs to persuade people to steer clear of alcohol. It encourages couples to have more children by offering better maternity pay. There are even awards for big families: parents with seven or more children receive an Order of Parental Glory!

≪ President Putin (center) presents the Order of Parental Glory to a family with seven children, in 2015.

9

A LAND OF CONTRASTS

The Ural Mountains run south to the Ural River.

As well as an incredible variety of scenery, Russia has every climate zone except tropical. In the summer, people lounge on the sunny beaches of the Black Sea. In contrast, the "Wild East" of Siberia is the coldest inhabited place in the world. Winter temperatures drop to a staggering -76°F (-60°C).

« Lake Baikal freezes from January to May or June.

Landscapes

Lake Baikal is the world's oldest and deepest freshwater lake: it's 5,387 feet (1,642 m) to the bottom—that's over a mile (1.6 km) deep! The longest river is the River Lena. The Ural Mountains straddle Russia from North to South for 1,600 miles (2,500 km), forming the boundary between Europe and Asia. All the known chemical elements on Earth are found there.

⌃ In the summer, people flock to the sunny beaches of the Black Sea.

FOCUS ON

☑ WINTER WARMERS

To venture out in the Siberian winter, wear a traditional shapka-ushanka. It's a cozy hat with flaps to pull down over your ears. You'll need a thick coat and warm boots too.

« A Russian fisherman dressed for the snowy weather with a fur-lined hat and boots.

∨ Evergreen coniferous trees in the taiga forests of Siberia.

Forests: the "lungs of Europe"

Half of Russia is covered by forests. In the North, the coniferous forests of the taiga range over a large part of Siberia. They absorb more carbon dioxide than all forests except the Amazon rain forest, and produce oxygen for our planet. Further north are the plains of the tundra, covered in permafrost—the soil is permanently frozen. The tundra is known as the "Land of the Midnight Sun" because it's always light in summer.

∨ Summer night in the northern tundra— it's light and there's snow on the ground.

LAKE BAIKAL IS SO LARGE THAT ALL THE RIVERS IN THE WORLD WOULD TAKE A YEAR TO FILL IT!

11

GO WILD IN RUSSIA

Russia's wildlife is adapted to survive in its extreme habitats. In the chilly tundra, mosses, lichens and grasses hug close to the ground. Arctic foxes have short, rounded ears to reduce heat loss and fur-covered soles to keep their feet cozy. A long, thick, shaggy coat of long brown hair protects musk oxen (right). Reindeer simply avoid the tundra winter by heading for the forests.

⌃ Arctic foxes turn white in winter for camouflage against the snow.

Taiga forest

The taiga woodlands are home to small mammals, including sable and ermine (weasels), and squirrels. Foxes, bears and wolves hunt elk and deer. Foxes and wolves also roam the steppes. There's little natural shelter, but marmots, mice and other burrowing animals can make a quick getaway from predators underground.

« Moose live in the floodplains (flat areas) of the taiga.

Lake Baikal

Lake Baikal is a unique habitat. It's home to the earless nerpa, the only seal that lives in freshwater. It can stay underwater for up to an hour and dive down to 1,000 feet (300 m). It's a mystery how seals reached Lake Baikal, hundreds of miles from the sea. Another unusual resident is the golomyanka fish; instead of laying eggs, it gives birth to live young.

« The extraordinary earless nerpa seal of Lake Baikal.

⌄ The grasslands, the vast grassy areas of southern Russia, are called the steppe.

AROUND TWO-THIRDS OF THE 1,700 SPECIES OF PLANTS AND ANIMALS IN LAKE BAIKAL ARE FOUND NOWHERE ELSE ON EARTH.

FOCUS ON

☑ SAVE THE SIBERIAN TIGER

The WWF Tiger Youth Forum is an international group of youth ambassadors who raise awareness among young people of the need to save the tigers. They protest against illegal hunting. In Russia, the Siberian tiger was dying out, but campaigners are pushing for the Tx2 goal to double numbers of wild tigers from 2010 to 2022.

» The number of Siberian tigers in Russia is rising again.

13

RICH RESOURCES

Russia is one of the world's fastest-growing economies. It is blessed with vast resources of oil, gas and minerals: coal, metals, diamonds and gold. Russia sells more gas than any other country and is the second largest oil exporter after Saudi Arabia. Russia has influence over other countries because they rely on its oil and gas supplies.

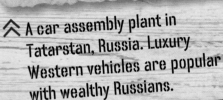

⊼ A car assembly plant in Tatarstan, Russia. Luxury Western vehicles are popular with wealthy Russians.

"Resource curse"

Yet Russia suffers from the "resource curse." Its economy yo-yos up and down with oil prices. In 2008, the world price of oil plummeted, and Russia was plunged into crisis. In 2011, oil prices rose again and the economy recovered. The government paid back some money it owed and unemployment fell. But prices swooped down again in 2015.

⌄ An oil tanker carries fuel from the oil fields of Siberia.

⌄ Oil pumps in Russia

Industry and services

Heavy industry is big business, especially metals, machine building, transport equipment and chemicals. Service industries are growing too—including tourism. Visitors cruise in steamships on the Volga River, enjoy bird watching around Lake Baikal or visit the country's world-class galleries and museums.

≪ The Hermitage Museum in St. Petersburg is Russia's largest art gallery.

OIL, GAS AND MINERALS MAKE UP FOUR-FIFTHS OF RUSSIA'S EXPORTS.

FOCUS ON

☑ EMISSIONS AND THE ENVIRONMENT

With all that heavy industry, Russia is the biggest producer of carbon dioxide emissions after China and the US. In 2015, it promised to reduce emissions by 25-30 percent below the 1990 level by 2030. However, climate experts say it must do more to clean up its act.

≪ Critics say Russian factory owners are not doing enough to prevent air pollution.

ON THE MOVE

Russia's major cities are gridlocked with traffic, but many areas of the country lack paved roads. Just a third of Russians have a car. People usually travel by train, and most goods trundle through the country on freight trains.

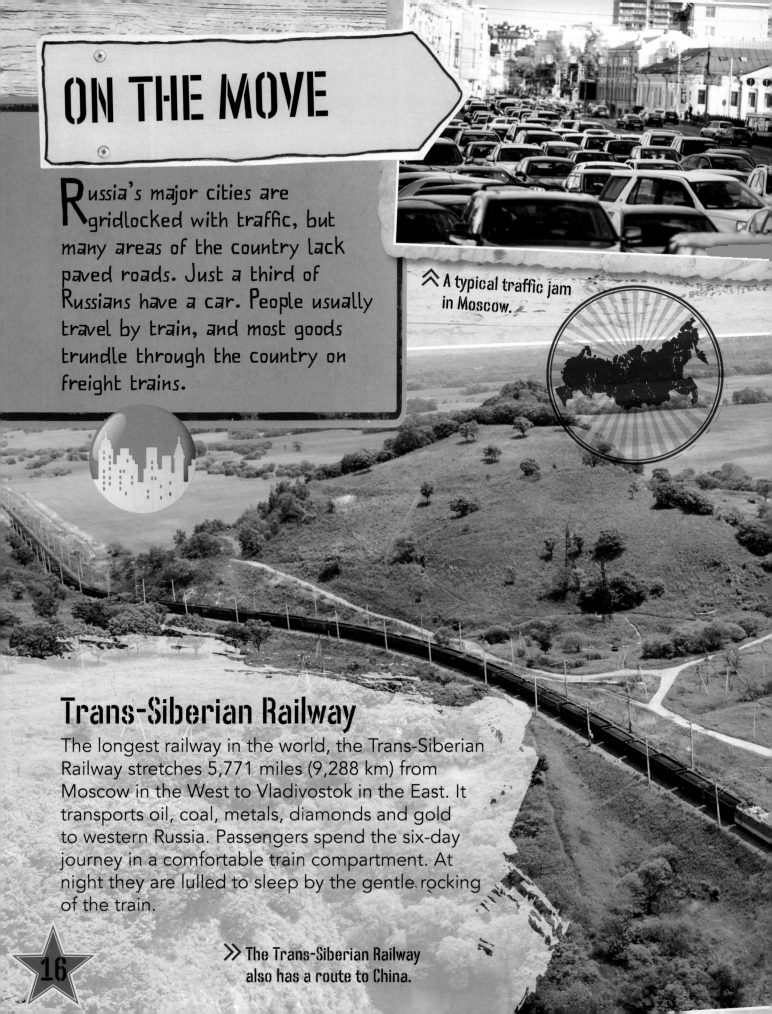

⌃ A typical traffic jam in Moscow.

Trans-Siberian Railway

The longest railway in the world, the Trans-Siberian Railway stretches 5,771 miles (9,288 km) from Moscow in the West to Vladivostok in the East. It transports oil, coal, metals, diamonds and gold to western Russia. Passengers spend the six-day journey in a comfortable train compartment. At night they are lulled to sleep by the gentle rocking of the train.

≫ The Trans-Siberian Railway also has a route to China.

EVERY DAY, THE MOSCOW METRO CARRIES MORE PEOPLE THAN THE LONDON AND NEW YORK METROS PUT TOGETHER.

Underground palaces

To get around Moscow and St. Petersburg, go underground. Moscow's speedy metro system carries an astounding 9.5 million passengers daily. The stations are richly decorated like palaces or museums. Their walls and columns are often made from colored marble and covered with paintings, mosaics and sculptures.

« Chandeliers glitter above the platforms at the beautiful Komsomolskaya Metro station in Moscow.

FOCUS ON

☑ SPACE RACE

Russia has been a leader in space technology since Soviet times. Yuri Gagarin was the first man to orbit Earth in 1961, and two years later, Valentina Tereshkova was the first woman in space. Nowadays, the Russian Space Agency promotes space tourism. If you have $18–37 million to spend, you could travel by spacecraft to the International Space Station, about 250 miles (400 km) above Earth.

« The Russian "Progress" spacecraft prepares for liftoff on a mission to carry cargo to the International Space Station in 2010.

ON THE LAND

↗ A welcome lunch break at a collective farm in the Kiev region, in 1936

Life on the land in most countries tends to change at a snail's pace — but not in Russia. Under Soviet rule, the collective farms had to hand over all their produce to the government. Farmers couldn't see the point of working hard only to give away all their crops, so the farms did badly. Now, many collective farms are run as companies or cooperatives.

From land and sea

Most farmland is used for raising crops. Wheat, barley, rye and oats fill the grasslands, while millet and melons grow along the lower River Volga. Beef cattle and pigs are kept for their meat. Russia has long coastlines, and fishing is a good source of income. With the largest forest reserves in the world, Russian loggers are busy exporting timber, paper and other wood products.

↗ A huge timber carrier transports logs. Russia has around one-quarter of all the world's trees.

≫ A fishing boat in Sochi, on the Black Sea coast

WITH MUCH OF RUSSIA'S TERRITORY A FROZEN WASTELAND, JUST 13 PERCENT OF THE LAND IS USED FOR AGRICULTURE.

All change

After a decade of decline in the 1990s, farming grew impressively. Since 2000, huge farms have developed, the biggest owned by foreign companies. There's a government scheme to modernize agriculture by 2020. It aims to attract more foreign businesses and to cultivate unused land.

≫ A herd of cattle on the banks of the River Volga

FOCUS ON

☑ GROW YOUR OWN

People in Russia have always enjoyed growing their own fruit and vegetables on a small plot. These plots often kept them alive under communism and are still popular today. Nearly two-thirds of people living in cities have a vegetable garden or an allotment at their dacha, or summer home.

≪ Elderly women often sell produce from their allotments by the roadside.

19

MODERNIZING MOSCOW

About three-quarters of Russians live in cities. The capital, Moscow, is Russia's largest city by far. With its brightly painted onion-shaped domes, St. Basil's Cathedral is easily the most famous building. The Kremlin has ornate cathedrals and grand palaces and is home to the president.

⌃ St. Basil's Cathedral is now a museum for tourists.

Building and business

In recent years, Moscow has been one big construction site. Old Soviet-era hotels have been knocked to the ground while the Cathedral of Christ the Savior has been rebuilt. The Moscow International Business Center, still under development, includes the Mercury City tower, the tallest tower in Europe at 1,112 feet (339 m). The Manezh shopping center has shot up next to Red Square, full of shops and restaurants.

≫ Shoppers at a traditional weekend vegetable market in Moscow.

Crowded communalki

Many new homes have also been built, but the surge in population means there's a shortage of housing. Most people occupy tiny flats in tall apartment blocks. Large numbers still live in communalki—Soviet-style apartments, where families have one bedroom each and share the kitchen and bathroom. Nowadays, most people want a private apartment even though it costs more.

⌄ The Krasnogorsk housing development — brand-new high-rise blocks packed closely together.

⌄ Moscow International Business Center, with the Mercury City tower on the far left

MOSCOW'S POPULATION IS 11.5 MILLION AND RISING.

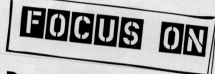

FOCUS ON

☑ RED SQUARE

Under Soviet rule, Moscow's Red Square was filled with thousands of soldiers parading in neat rows to celebrate Workers' Day on May 1. In 2008, the celebration was restored, but for Victory Day on May 9, to mark the end of World War II.

⌃ Victory Day fireworks light up Red Square.

ST. PETERSBURG

Russia's second largest city, St. Petersburg, was the country's capital for two centuries until the Russian Revolution (see pages 6-7). Less than half the size of Moscow, it's a significant historical and cultural center and a major port. St. Petersburg is known as "Venice of the North," after the Italian city built on a network of canals. It too has many canals, and no fewer than 342 bridges.

A ballet performance at the Mariinsky Theater in St. Petersburg.

City of culture

Peter the Great's successors brought European architects to design elegant palaces and cathedrals, so the city is full of beautiful historic buildings. The magnificent Hermitage Museum houses some of the world's greatest art collections. St. Petersburg also has the best of Russian contemporary art and it's the place for top-class ballet and opera.

The extraordinary Hermitage Museum, which houses a mind-boggling 3 million items!

Dvors

St. Petersburg is an intriguing mix of old and new. Huge modern shopping centers have been constructed in recent years. But step through arched entrances on the main streets and you can find yourself in a dvor—an old-fashioned enclosed courtyard, with buildings unchanged for decades.

« A view of the sky from an enclosed courtyard — some dvors connect one to another.

« A view of St. Isaac's Cathedral in St. Petersburg. The canals in the city center are lined with Italian-style mansions to add to the likeness with Venice.

LOOKING AT EVERY EXHIBIT IN THE HERMITAGE FOR A MINUTE WOULD TAKE 11 YEARS!

FOCUS ON

☑ WHITE NIGHTS

During the long summer evenings, it barely gets dark at night. On these White Nights, festivals are held in the concert halls, and everyone parties until late.

« People enjoy salsa dancing as part of a White Nights festival in St. Petersburg.

RAISED IN RUSSIA

Russian children can consider themselves lucky they didn't grow up in Soviet times. Rote learning was common – teachers expected pupils to memorize lots of facts. Nowadays, they encourage creative thinking so children can solve problems.

Study and training

Children start school at age seven. At 16, they decide whether to carry on with academic subjects and study for another two or three years for their secondary-level certificate. If they're eager to learn a trade instead, they can switch to vocational (work-based) training.

⋙ Even young primary school children sit formally at desks in rows.

⌃ As well as the basic subjects, children can do art at school.

⌃ Schools are investing in computers— these children are making a robot.

MOST RUSSIAN CHILDREN WEAR A SCHOOL UNIFORM.

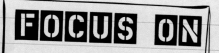

FOCUS ON

☑ ## FAVORITE ACTIVITIES

Gymnastics and ballet are top choices. Children start ballet at five and often dance alongside adults in performances. Many young people sing in a "xop" (say "hop") or choir, sometimes performing in traditional costume. They sing everything from classical pieces to folk and pop. Chess is taken seriously in Russia; lots of children join clubs and compete in tournaments.

⌃ Playing chess on the streets at a sports society celebration in Moscow.

⌃ Joining a sports club is popular. These boys are competing at a stadium event.

The school day

The school day is from 8 a.m. until 1 or 2 p.m. Main subjects include Russian literature and language, math, history, geography, the sciences and physical education. Children from ethnic minorities study in their own language but learn Russian at secondary school. After school, there's a choice of extra activities, including dancing, sports, singing, painting and crafts. Many children attend Youth Club after school, on the weekend, and on school holidays to make friends and learn new skills.

CHILLING OUT

» You can go skiing or snowboarding at one of Russia's many ski resorts.

Winter weather doesn't stop Russians from having fun. They take to the ice and go skating, skiing and sledding. Ice hockey is popular too. Players wear a helmet because this fast-moving sport can be dangerous — no one wants to fall and crack their head on the ice.

> ICE HOCKEY IS ONE OF RUSSIA'S FAVORITE SPORTS, AND THE NATIONAL TEAM IS HIGHLY SUCCESSFUL.

» The competition is fierce in this ice hockey tournament.

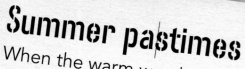

Summer pastimes

When the warm weather finally comes, people head outdoors to enjoy tennis, jogging or swimming. They walk in the countryside or fish in the lakes. Elderly people play chess and dominoes in the park.

« Children in giant transparent balls enjoy zorbing on a lake in Novgorod.

26

>> Russians love to spend time tending their vegetable patches.

Days at the dacha

Although more Russians vacation abroad than they used to, the majority have a "staycation." Most families in cities have access to a dacha—a wooden summer house by a lake, river or the sea. They spend their summer holidays there, growing fruit and vegetables, enjoying the fresh air and having barbecues. Often, there's no running water so they get it from a well or village pump.

FOCUS ON

☑ STORYTELLING

The long, dark evenings create the perfect atmosphere for storytelling. A favorite character in children's fairy tales is witch Baba Yaga, who lives in a house raised on chicken legs and flies around in a mortar (heavy bowl), scaring people. Many fairy tales were collected and written down by the poet Alexsandr Pushkin (1799–1837).

<< A sculpture of Baba Yaga; in stories she is wise and powerful as well as scary.

27

RELIGIOUS REVIVAL

Under communism, religion was banned and it was impossible to follow Christian customs openly. Since Russia's independence, there's been a huge surge in religious fervor among all ages. Old churches have been repaired and many new ones built. Like churches, mosques have mushroomed since 1991, when there were only 300. By 2015 there were more than 8,000. Islam is Russia's second most popular religion.

A spiritual experience

On Sunday, bells from the splendid blue- or gold-domed Orthodox church call the people to prayer. In the decorative interior, the atmosphere is warm and inviting. Hundreds of people pack into the church and go to kiss icons and light candles in front of them. It's all part of the spiritual experience of the Orthodox Church. After the service, people take home bottles of holy water, which they believe cure all manner of illnesses.

» Opened in 2015, Moscow Cathedral Mosque is the city's main mosque.

« Trinity Lavra, near Moscow, the most important monastery (monks' home) of the Russian Orthodox Church — with typical blue and gold domes.

ABOUT 10–15 PERCENT OF THE RUSSIAN POPULATION ARE MUSLIMS.

≪ Most Christians are members of the Russian Orthodox Church. Everyone stands for the church service, which involves lots of singing.

⤊ The priest blesses the worshipers with holy water.

FOCUS ON

☑ ICONS

Russian Orthodox churches have a solid screen decorated with icons — religious paintings, usually on wood, showing scenes from the Bible or the lives of saints. These holy objects are a vital element in worship. On festival days, the priest and worshipers carry icons in a procession around the church.

⤊ Lighting candles helps people to feel a personal link with God.

29

FESTIVAL FUN

New Year is Russia's biggest festival. On New Year's Eve, families gather for a special dinner. At 11:55 p.m., the president addresses the nation. The Kremlin clock chimes at midnight (main picture), the national anthem plays, and in cities, fireworks light up the night sky.

⌃ Musicians on a street stage during the Pancake Week celebrations.

Christmas

Religious festivals have made a huge comeback. Orthodox Christmas is celebrated on January 7. The night before, people eat a delicious rich meal of 12 dishes, called Holy Supper.

⌃ People gather in Moscow to celebrate Christmas Eve.

RUSSIAN CHILDREN RECEIVE NEW YEAR'S GIFTS FROM GRANDFATHER FROST AND THE SNOW MAIDEN, THE RUSSIAN VERSION OF SANTA CLAUS.

Pancake feasts

Maslenitsa (Pancake Week) is a week of feasting before Lent. It's a time for snowball fights, sleigh rides, celebrations and dancing in traditional costumes and, of course, eating pancakes. These tasty treats are eaten to celebrate the start of spring. The shape of the pancake stands for the sun. Russians enjoy their pancakes with sour cream, melted butter, jam or caviar (fish eggs).

>> Pancakes served with caviar, sour cream and jam — delicious!

FOCUS ON

☑ EASTER EGGS

Easter eggs aren't always made from chocolate! In Russia, people exchange beautifully decorated eggs at Easter. Some are real ones, dipped in colorful dye. Others are made from wood, painted with flowers, churches or bright patterns.

>> One of the famous Easter eggs made by jeweler Peter Carl Fabergé (1846–1920) for the royal family.

31

COUNTRY OF CULTURE

Russia is famous for its top-notch literature, theater, classical music, ballet and art. Perhaps you've heard of Leo Tolstoy's *Anna Karenina* (1875-7) or his epic *War and Peace* (1865-9), made into a BBC TV drama in 2015. Fyodor Dostoevsky wrote the gripping detective story *Crime and Punishment* (1866).

∧ A portrait of the author Leo Tolstoy, in 1873.

19th-century classics

Check the performances at a major theater or concert hall, and it's likely a great 19th-century Russian work will appear. Anton Chekhov is famous for his realistic plays, including *The Seagull* (1896) and *The Cherry Orchard* (1904). His strong characters struggled to cope with the changes in their lives and society. People can still relate to those issues today. Piotr Ilich Tchaikovsky (1840–93) is probably Russia's best-known composer.

« An abstract painting by one of Russia's best-known artists, Vasily Kandinsky (1866–1944), on a French stamp.

∧ Keira Knightley starred in a film of *Anna Karenina* in 2012.

✓ BEAUTIFUL BALLET

Ballet was introduced to Russia in the 17th century to entertain the tsar. Russian enthusiasm for this dance form grew, and by the 20th century, Russian ballet companies were touring the world. Today, you have to grab tickets for the hugely successful Bolshoi and Mariinsky Ballet months in advance.

∧ Tchaikovsky wrote the music for ballets including *Swan Lake* (above), *Sleeping Beauty* and *The Nutcracker*.

> MUSIC FROM TCHAIKOVSKY'S NUTCRACKER SUITE FEATURED IN THE 1940 DISNEY ANIMATED FILM FANTASIA.

Communist control

Under Soviet rule, artists and playwrights could not express themselves freely. They were expected to show the glorious march of communism, with strong workers happily tilling the land and laboring in the factories. The grip of Soviet control on the arts loosened in the 1980s.

⌄ An old statue of laborers dating back to the Soviet era.

∧ Aleksandr Solzhenitsyn (1918–2008) was forced into exile for writing books that criticized the government.

NEW RUSSIA, NEW CULTURE

Since the fall of the Soviet Union, a world of new Russian culture has opened up. To promote the country's new image, the government encourages Russian writers. The top literature competition is the Russian Booker Prize with a generous prize for the winner. The Read Russia organization publishes Russian authors in other languages.

⌃ Traditional matryoshka — Russian dolls — including ones of President Putin.

New writers

METRO2033 WAS TURNED INTO AN XBOX VIDEO GAME.

From the 1990s, writers such as Aleksandra Marinina and Viktor Dotsenko set their stories in the shadowy underworld of Russia's gangs. Marinina's novels have a strong female detective lead, Anastasia Kamenskaya. Fantasy and sci-fi have taken off too. Dmitrii Glukhovskii's *Metro2033* depicts a future dystopia (horrible world) where everyone lives in the Metro because nuclear war has destroyed the world above.

⌄ Marinina's novels were turned into a popular TV series.

New music

New Russian music has exploded onto the scene. Singer-songwriter Nyusha and the rock band Slot are big stars, yet they're barely known outside Russia. Even there, most young people listen to Western music. In contrast, some of the world's best classical musicians come from Russia.

⌃ Girl band Propaganda perform onstage in a Moscow club.

⌄ Opened in 2015, Garace Contemporary Culture Center is in Gorky Park, Moscow.

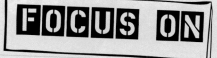

FOCUS ON

☑ GOING TO THE MOVIES

Government funding for filmmaking disappeared along with the Soviet Union. Since 2005, the Russian film industry has revived, with some government support. Multiscreen complexes have sprouted up in major cities, and cinema audiences are growing. But it's foreign films most people come to see, especially the latest Hollywood blockbusters.

⌃ Moscow International Film Festival is held every year and awards prizes to some of the world's top filmmakers.

35

CRAZY FOR SPORTS

In the days of communism, the Soviet government promoted sports to show the superiority of its political system. Although communism is long gone, Russians are as enthusiastic about sports as ever.

Medal winners

Russia has enjoyed incredible success in gymnastics, tennis and athletics. Talented young gymnasts go to Moscow Children's Palace of Culture and Sport for training. Maria Sharapova was the first Russian to win Wimbledon in 2004, at just 17. Since 1996, Russia has won more medals at the Olympic Games than all other countries except the US. But in 2015, Russia was banned from international athletics competitions, accused of allowing athletes to use drugs to improve their performance.

AFTER THE 2012 OLYMPICS, ALL 129 RUSSIAN MEDALISTS WERE GIVEN A BRAND–NEW AUDI CAR.

《 Maria Sharapova

⌃ A talented young gymnast in training at the Dynamo club in Moscow.

Soccer fanatics

Soccer is the top spectator sport in Russia. Favorite clubs include Zenit from St. Petersburg and its rival Dynamo from Moscow. Kids dream of playing for one of these teams. Wealthy Russians have pumped money into major clubs to buy foreign players and managers to up their game, and have purchased foreign clubs. In 2003, Roman Abramovich bought English club Chelsea. Russia will host the FIFA World Cup in 2018.

FOCUS ON

☑ SOCHI 2014

In 2014, Russia hosted the Winter Olympics in the southern city of Sochi. The competition was held against a background of poor management, corruption, security threats and political unrest in nearby Ukraine. In the end, the event passed off peacefully, and Russia won the most medals.

⩔ The Olympic Park in Sochi, just before the opening ceremony of the 2014 Olympics.

⩓ Russia's Mariya Savinova expresses her joy as she wins the gold medal in the women's 800 meters final at the London 2012 Olympics.

37

BLINIS AND BORSCHT

Living in a chilly climate, Russians love warming foods with plenty of carbs. They eat hot, filling dishes, usually home-cooked with locally grown beetroot, cabbage and potatoes. Russians eat potatoes most days, and there's always dark, chewy rye bread on the table. Alongside traditional fare are modern Russian dishes, influenced by French cooking. Fast food is popular, especially burgers, pizza and hot dogs.

⌃ Pickled vegetables, including chiles, peppers and cucumbers, on sale at a farmers' market.

RUSSIANS ADORE PICKLED ZAKUSKI (APPETIZERS) SUCH AS PICKLED CUCUMBERS, MUSHROOMS AND HERRING.

Hearty food

For a traditional Russian breakfast, people eat kasha (porridge), a sandwich, eggs or cereal. Lunch is the main meal. Many cafes and restaurants offer a cheap lunchtime menu: soup, meat with potatoes or porridge, and tea or coffee. Families gather for dinner around 7 p.m., often in front of the TV. Dinner is usually a meat dish, perhaps with Russian salad, made from potatoes, mayonnaise and vegetables. It's followed by a cup of sweet tea.

>> A bowl of tasty borscht.

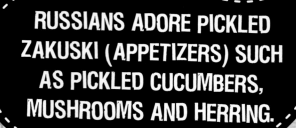

<< Russian
salad

Top treats
Other popular dishes include borscht, a deep red beetroot soup eaten hot or cold with sour cream, dill and rye bread. Blinis are thin pancakes with butter, sour cream, jam or caviar added for flavor.

⌄ A batch of blinis served with caviar and sour cream.

⌃ Pelmeni (dumplings) can be stuffed with meat, fish or mushrooms.

<< A modern electric samovar

FOCUS ON

☑ THE SAMOVAR

In the old days, Russians lit charcoal under this metal urn to heat water for drinking tea whenever they wanted. A stand on top kept the teapot hot. Nowadays, many people use electric samovars or kettles.

RULING RUSSIA

Russia's government has undergone extraordinary changes. After the Soviet state crumbled, there were the beginnings of democracy—lots of new political parties popped up. Yet within just a few years, a powerful leader ruled Russia once again.

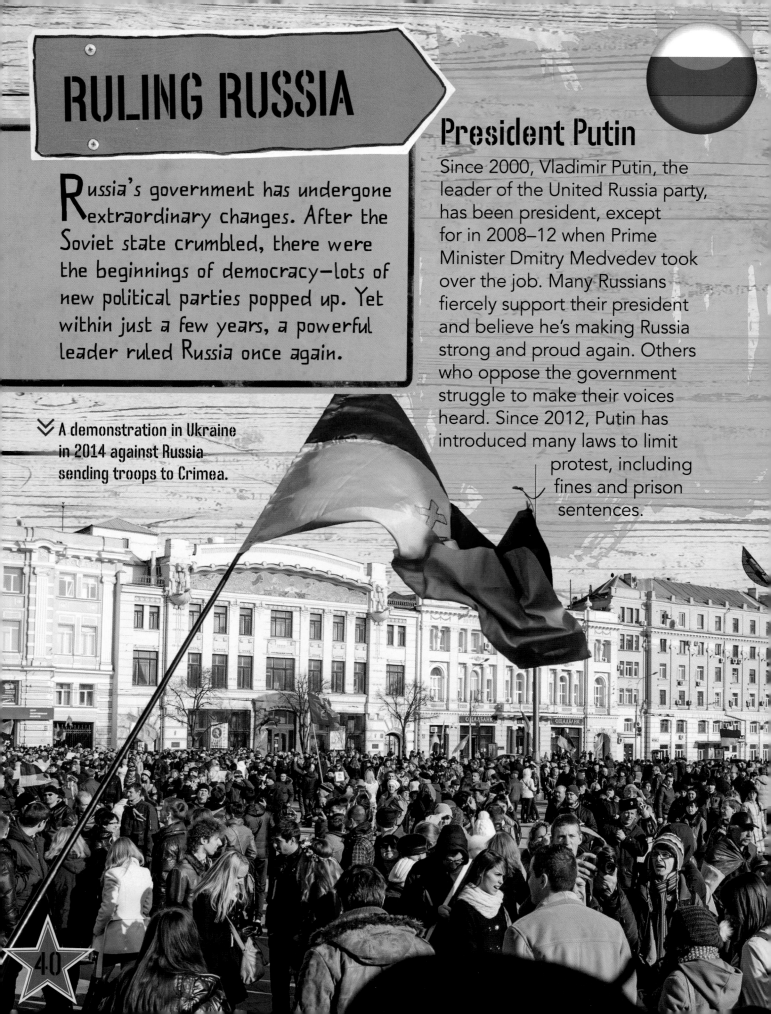

A demonstration in Ukraine in 2014 against Russia sending troops to Crimea.

President Putin

Since 2000, Vladimir Putin, the leader of the United Russia party, has been president, except for in 2008–12 when Prime Minister Dmitry Medvedev took over the job. Many Russians fiercely support their president and believe he's making Russia strong and proud again. Others who oppose the government struggle to make their voices heard. Since 2012, Putin has introduced many laws to limit protest, including fines and prison sentences.

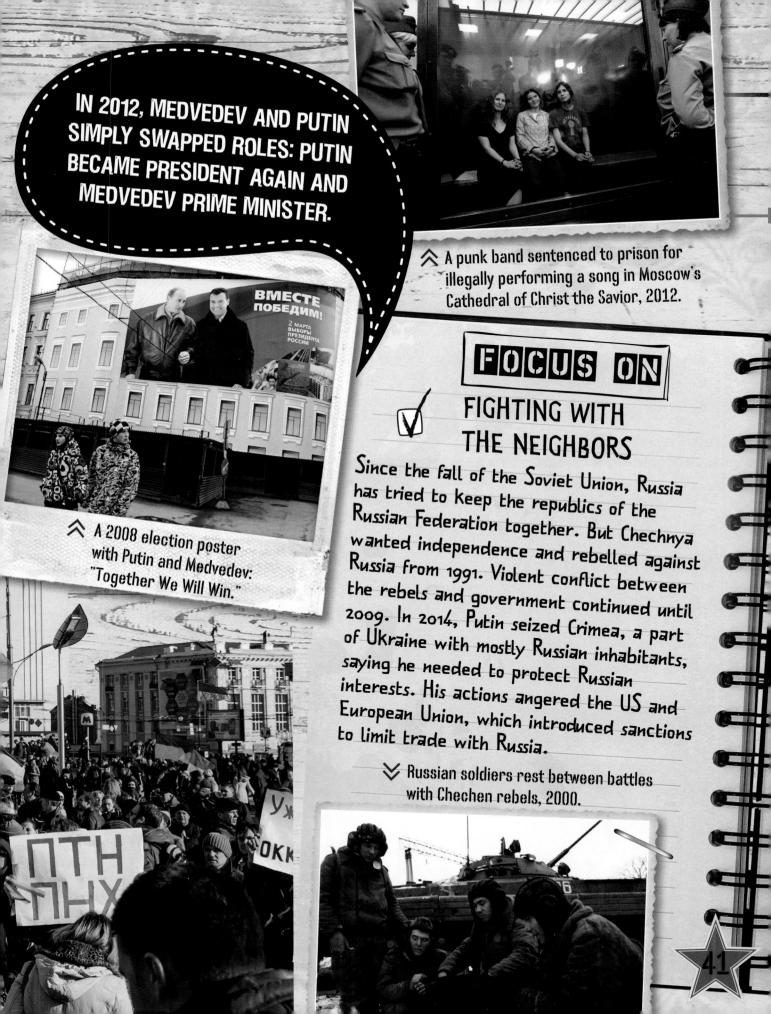

IN 2012, MEDVEDEV AND PUTIN SIMPLY SWAPPED ROLES: PUTIN BECAME PRESIDENT AGAIN AND MEDVEDEV PRIME MINISTER.

A 2008 election poster with Putin and Medvedev: "Together We Will Win."

⟰ A punk band sentenced to prison for illegally performing a song in Moscow's Cathedral of Christ the Savior, 2012.

FOCUS ON

✓ FIGHTING WITH THE NEIGHBORS

Since the fall of the Soviet Union, Russia has tried to keep the republics of the Russian Federation together. But Chechnya wanted independence and rebelled against Russia from 1991. Violent conflict between the rebels and government continued until 2009. In 2014, Putin seized Crimea, a part of Ukraine with mostly Russian inhabitants, saying he needed to protect Russian interests. His actions angered the US and European Union, which introduced sanctions to limit trade with Russia.

⟱ Russian soldiers rest between battles with Chechen rebels, 2000.

THE "RUSSIAN IDEA"

Russians are proud of their nation and values and have a strong sense of identity. They believe in their spiritual existence, sense of community and links with the land. For example, they keep up the age-old tradition of picking mushrooms and berries in the countryside. Most Russians feel they should keep up their traditions but also borrow from the "best of the West."

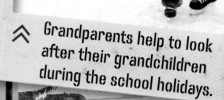

⌃ Grandparents help to look after their grandchildren during the school holidays.

Winter sports

The cold climate is part of Russian identity. When the lakes freeze over, people go ice fishing and skating. They love skiing. For the truly brave, there's ice swimming. Known as morzhi (walruses), ice swimmers cut holes in the ice so they can immerse themselves in freezing-cold water. Brrrh!

⌃ People travel from the cities to pick mushrooms.

RUSSIA HAS MORE THAN 200 KINDS OF EDIBLE MUSHROOMS, BUT WATCH OUT FOR THE POISONOUS ONES!

Hot baths

To warm up, you can visit a Russian banya (sauna), another essential Russian experience. It's thought that the hot, damp steam helps to expel fat from the body and clean the skin.

>> The birch brooms in the banya are for smacking cold water onto your body.

⌄ An ice swimmer bravely bathing in a hole in the ice.

FOCUS ON

✓ THE DOWNSIDE

Some take pride in their nation to extremes and exclude others, calling for "Russia for the Russians." Far-right groups have carried out attacks on immigrants, unfairly blaming them for the increase in crime in cities. And some believe that Russian values don't include accepting lesbian and gay people. In 2013, a law was passed against homosexuality. This has fueled a rise in attacks on lesbians and gays.

⌃ People protest in support of lesbian and gay rights in St. Petersburg, 2015.

43

LOOKING TO THE FUTURE

The heat's definitely on for Russia; climate change is a major challenge. Higher temperatures could melt the Siberian permafrost — handy for growing more food. But wilder weather could bring disastrous droughts and floods.

Renewable energy

The government is beginning to address climate change. In 2015, it introduced new measures to encourage the growth of renewable energy such as wind and solar power. Electricity companies were told to buy from renewable sources.

⩘ A heatwave in 2010 brought devastating forest and peat fires.

≫ Tourists visiting Intercession Cathedral in Red Square, Moscow in 2010. The city is covered in dense smoke from the burning forests.

≪ A mini solar power plant in a Moscow park. In 2015, many new solar projects were approved.

⌃ Nearly everyone in Russia has at least one mobile phone.

Normal life

Despite upheavals and rapid change in Russia, most people live a "normal" Western-style life. Two-thirds have jobs in service industries and a quarter work in industry. Around half the population use the Internet every day, and they love social media. Russians in the 21st century are likely to have a similar lifestyle to people in other developed countries.

⌄ Young people watch a show about electricity and magnetism at a science festival in St. Petersburg.

SEVENTY PERCENT OF 17- TO 22-YEAR-OLDS GO TO UNIVERSITY IN RUSSIA, COMPARED TO ABOUT 40 PERCENT IN THE USA.

45

QUIZ

H ow much do you know about Russia's land and people? Try this quick quiz and find out!

4 What do most Russians do in the summer holidays?
a) Go on holiday abroad
b) Stay at home
c) Go to a dacha in the countryside

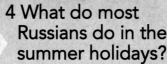

5 Where is St. Basil's Cathedral?
a) St. Petersburg
b) Moscow
c) Siberia

1 Which climate zone is not found in Russia?
a) Tundra
b) Tropical
c) Taiga

2 What are blinis?
a) Pickled cucumbers
b) Appetizers
c) Thin pancakes

3 What's unique about Lake Baikal?
a) Many of the species there are found nowhere else on Earth.
b) It's a long way from the sea.
c) It has freshwater.

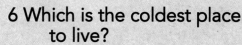

6 Which is the coldest place to live?
a) Siberia
b) St. Petersburg
c) The Black Sea

7 When do Russians celebrate Orthodox Christmas?
a) January 7
b) December 24
c) December 25

8 Who was Anton Chekhov?
a) A famous composer
b) A 19th-century artist
c) A popular playwright

True or false?
1) You can go by train from Russia to China.
2) The Ural Mountains are the highest in the world.
3) Nearly everyone in Russia has a car.

Answers: 1b, 2c, 3a, 4c, 5b, 6a, 7a, 8c; True or False? 1T, 2F, 3F

GLOSSARY

ambassador
A person who speaks on behalf of an international organization or their country.

civil war
War between groups in the same country.

communist
A system in which the government owns and controls the means of production, such as farms and mines.

contemporary
Belonging to the present time.

cooperative
A business owned and run by the people involved, with the profits shared by them.

corruption
When people in charge behave dishonestly.

democracy
A political system in which all adults can vote in free elections for the rulers of the country.

emissions
Light, heat or gases that are sent out into the atmosphere.

empire
A group of countries that are controlled by one country.

ethnic group
A group of people who share a culture, tradition, way of life and sometimes language.

freight
Goods that are transported by ships, planes, trucks or trains.

immigrant
A person who moves to settle in another country.

life expectancy
The number of years that a person is likely to live.

permafrost
A layer of soil that is permanently frozen, in very cold regions of the world.

renewable energy
Energy that is replaced naturally, such as energy from the wind and sun.

republic
A country ruled by a president.

revolution
When a group of people organize to change the government of a country.

sanctions
An official order that limits trade and contacts with a particular country, in order to make it do something, such as obeying international law.

superpower
A country that has very great military or economic power and a lot of influence.

taiga
Forest that grows in wet ground in far northern regions of the earth.

time zone
One of the 24 areas that the world is divided into, each with its own time.

tundra
The large, flat Arctic regions of northern Europe, Asia and North America.

Further information

Books

Countries Around the World: Russia by Jilly Hunt (Heinemann, 2012)

Developing World: Russia and Moscow by Philip Steele (Franklin Watts, 2016)

It's Cool to Learn About Countries: Russia by Katie Marsico (Kindle Edition; Cherry Lake Publishing, 2013)

R is for Russia by Vladimir Kabakov (Frances Lincoln Children's Books, 2013)

Russia: A Benjamin Blog and His Inquisitive Dog Guide by Anita Ganeri (Raintree, 2015)

Websites

www.activityvillage.co.uk/russia
Activity village: Russia

www.timeforkids.com/destination/russia
TIME for kids Russia

www.oxfam.org.uk/education/resources/your-world-my-world
Explores the lives of four children around the world, including Russia

Index